Your Greatest Good

How Changing Yourself Can Change the World

Your Greatest Good

How Changing Yourself Can Change the World

James R Scheu

© 2019 James R Scheu

ISBN 978-0-35987-463-7

Library of Congress Case Number: 1-7965572731

15218 Summit Avenue

Ste 300-723

Fontana, CA 92336

Please forward any correspondence, request for information, or comments to the above address. Alternatively, please be sure to follow James' blog at nlabca.org

Cover Design by sabrina ihadadene

Interior Design by James R Scheu

Editing by Simon Behan

Printed in the USA

For my wife who continues to see something in me, and gives me the courage to consistently pursue a better version of myself.

And for my children, whom I seek change within myself that I may be a better dad and change within the world that they may have a better future.

"When I was a young man, I wanted to change the world.

I found it difficult to change the world,

so I tried to change my nation.

When I found I could not change the nation,

I began to focus on my town.

I could not change the town and as an older man,

I tried to change my family.

Now as an old man, I realize the only thing I can change is myself,

and suddenly I realize that if long ago I had changed myself,

I could have made an impact on my family.

My family and I could have made an impact on our town.

Their impact could have changed the nation

and I could indeed have changed the world."

Unknown Monk, 1100 A.D.

TABLE OF CONTENTS

Greater Good Defined — 11

Introduction — 15

Section One: Mindful Preparation — 27
    Deciding on Altruism — 31
    Finding Your Purpose — 43
    Creating a Vision — 57

Section Two: Intentional Action — 65
    Be Intentional — 67
    Your Character is Who You Are — 77
    Be Courageous — 107
    Stop Talking, Start Acting — 119

Section Three: Perpetual Perseverance — 139
    Be Resilient — 141
    Be Disciplined — 157
    Find Your Tribe — 165

Closing Thought — 177

Acknowledgments — 179

Greater Good Defined

"The 'greater good' is defined here as a good that positively impacts the greater number of communities, rather than the special interests of individuals, smaller groups, or of the policy makers themselves. It requires an acknowledgment and respect for diversity, an aim for genuine efforts towards inclusivity, and collective actions that are bound by the objective of equity. Equity, not to be confused with equality, is when all people have what they need to reach the same opportunities for choice, health, prosperity, and well-being.

For me, this means that no person can be denied access to these essential goods because they belong to no one, and therefore, they are the rights of everyone. The common goods include clean air and water, shelter, safety and access to education. In addition, all people should be empowered to pursue knowledge that lets them grow, to live healthy, to live free.

It takes collective action to address the issues that create the most inequities. In the context of this book, however, the "greatest good" is our individual ability and readiness to effect change within ourselves so that we are adequately prepared to tackle these issues and effect positive change for the collective."

INTRODUCTION

The current social environment we reside in, a stale, static state of progress, with few, sporadic jolts of impact, is largely due to a fatal flaw that continues to threaten significant transformational change initiatives, hindering the possibility of any real or meaningful success. The flaw is a simple one, seemingly obvious, and yet, is also the greatest potential asset. It is critical to the success of any change initiative and, yet, is the most overlooked and underestimated aspect. What is this flaw? Simply stated; 'people'.

Having worked as a firefighter for more than fifteen years, first in the military and then as a civilian, I found a renewed sense of passion when working to bring transformational change. Leading several multi-sector change initiatives, working alongside business partners and community members, and discovering the joy in helping people change their lives is an intoxicating and immensely satisfying feeling. On those projects I encountered many leaders along the way, good people trying to make meaningful change in places that mattered to them. This book is for them.

The leaders I've met go out there every day and do everything they can to enhance their communities. They have a genuine drive and passion for making things better, for leaving the world a little better than they found it. But those leaders face what seem like insurmountable odds: funding, bureaucracy, red tape, not to mention cronyism and corruption. I've faced those challenges myself – and lost.

But this book is not about defeat. It's not even about victory. It's about committing every day to getting better, to becoming more, to evolving. It's about accepting the challenges in front of you and realizing that sometimes the obstacle is actually the way forward. In my experiences, the only solution I had was to grow. In doing so, I was able to develop tools that helped me become a more effective agent of change. What I write down here is an attempt to use my experiences to give leaders some insights that may help them help others.

From challenges that seemed, and sometimes were, insurmountable.

How it all began

In early 2018, I was managing a regional multi-sector coalition to reduce the incidence rate of diabetes in the Inland Empire of Southern California. After nearly two years into the project, we were making considerable progress despite an ambitious project goal and timeline. However, I began to receive pressure from outside the project, to steer many of the project objectives and goals in a decidedly different direction; one that favored the interests and of hospital and healthcare organizations over the benefit of the community we were charged with serving. With the pressure coming from within my own organization, rather than bend and fold to save my job and livelihood, I chose to remain committed to my principles and maintain the integrity of our cause. I took definitive steps to block the outside meddling, shield the project members, and address the improprieties within my own organization. Ultimately, I was unceremoniously terminated in an effort by the board to contain and conceal the bullying, self-dealing and misappropriations they had allowed from their own chair for so many years.

During those months, I was afraid. I was an emotional wreck. The situation took a heavy toll on my mental health and physical wellbeing - took more than a year to heal and recover from. But it also provided amazing lessons that I could not have learned if I had made different choices; choices that would not have allowed me to hold my head high and maintain a clear conscience. However, I still look back with pride because I had the courage to stand for what I believe in. I refused to allow cronyism and corruption to go unchecked.

The missing link

As I worked on large-scale community health improvement initiatives, I began to slowly understand what worked, what was important, and what led to the greatest impact for the communities we were serving. I also realized what was missing from the existing frameworks for facilitating multi-sector partnerships. From these learning's and experiences, my partners and I began to develop a new type of framework that would ensure inclusivity, that community was central to decision-making, and that equity was an intentional outcome rather than an afterthought.

As I reflected on the challenges and barriers to the work, I realized that the most common reason for failure was not because the ideas were bad, or the solutions were poorly planned. It was most often due to the individuals being unaware, unprepared, unable, or unwilling to effectively lead. In order for change initiatives to work, no matter how large or small, the scale, scope, and concept are all irrelevant if the individuals that make up the team's leading the efforts are not equipped to handle the pressures and challenges of the change process.

But as a nonprofit leader, I saw the challenges with funding, bureaucracy and red tape that stymies progress and frustrates sector leaders who genuinely want to do the right thing for their communities. I also experienced firsthand the corruption of personal interests, shady business ventures, and back-door dealings that are becoming all too common in today's corporate and societal landscape. The systems and structures, and certainly improper behaviors, present significant challenges for leaders that have a genuine desire and passion for improving conditions that lead to better health and wellbeing of communities and leaving the world a little better than they found it. Leaders need help.

A new mindset

My work, like that of many others, is largely about relationships. It focuses a good portion of time on building and fostering relationships that are rooted in honesty, trust, compassion, and integrity. Too often, we rush through life and network with people and organizations solely to advance a business, sealing the next deal, or climbing the next rung on the ladder to success. And while that may be sufficient for some, it does not provide inward reflection, self-improvement, and self-awareness to confront the motivations for our business actions, which all too often is simply a desire for more.

Sometimes progress means boldly facing your fear of the unknown and marching through the fog of anxiety. These moments help us understand that the greatest value is the experience of learning and growing, not necessarily from success or achievement. When you embrace the beauty of imperfection, you'll realize that striving for perfection is like chasing a unicorn.

Following my departure, my organization's newly appointed leadership swiftly moved in and attempted to take on my role in the coalition. Their desire to be seen as the experts, and revered as the "savior", meant that their solution and approach had to be perfect. The insecurity that arose from this blind pursuit had a negative impact on the coalition and the initiative was effectively diluted to something far less innovative and transformational from the original intended outcome. When we become too focused on perfection, or our own perception of what perfect looks like, we can quickly lose sight of what is important. Ultimately, we will become disenchanted, frustrated and become less energized in our pursuits. When you become frustrated and frozen in fear, the world continues on without you.

About this book

Many of the points in this book (actually, all of them!) are hard lessons that I myself had to learn, and the learning continues each day. They have left scrapes, bumps, and bruises; lasting impressions of the perils, difficulties and hazards I have endured. But they also constructed the armor that has built up my strength, resiliency, and ability to anticipate potential barriers in order to pursue the impossible dream of bringing meaningful change to communities, leaving a lasting impact on people, and caring about the greater good as I define it.

At times, these issues seem insurmountable and impossible for one person to change. But change is inevitable and large-scale change is possible. Not just a simple change of policy or practice within an organization or an approval by an executive board or bureaucratic council. Significant social conditions like poverty, hunger, and housing can be affected by each of us, and all of us, and you.

Before we, as a group, however, can come together to change the world, we must first be prepared within ourselves. Our thoughts about who we are, our abilities, our ideas, and our power to evolve are shaped by those who have come before us. We owe it to them and ourselves to pick up and carry the torch they ignited. The shared consciousness and cultural intelligence our mentors have forged should be a source of inspiration as we inherit the responsibility to influence and impact the world around us.

This book has been organized to lead you through a natural progression of personal transformation within three distinct areas:

- **Mindful Preparation**: the first step is always awareness
- **Intentional Action**: once aware, we need to implement our intentions with actions
- **Perpetual Perseverance**: once we start…we don't stop

Each of the following section will identify characteristics, behaviors, thoughts and practices that are singularly simple, but so powerful when combined and put to action. I urge you, and the change maker inside of you, to take what is offered here as an opportunity to learn, grow and expand your knowledge to unlock the incredible and infinite potential that resides within you.

Whether your goal is to be a part of solving world peace, to impact your community, or to simply improve your own standard of being, I invite you to read with intention, proceed with an open mind and embrace the information with your whole heart.

I am on a journey. A powerful one. An important one. Along the way I have needed constant advice and guidance. Maybe the lessons I've learned can help others along the way on theirs journey, even if it is simply to recognize the universal challenges of doing something meaningful and important. I wish you the best.

MINDFUL PREPARATION

"It is not the critic who counts;

not the man who points out how the strong man stumbles,
or where the doer of deeds could have done them better.
The credit belongs to the man who is actually in the arena,
whose face is marred by dust and sweat and blood;
who strives valiantly;
who errs, who comes short again and again,
because there is no effort without error and shortcoming;
but who does actually strive to do the deeds;
who knows great enthusiasms, the great devotions;
who spends himself in a worthy cause;
who at the best knows in the end the triumph of high achievement,
and who at the worst, if he fails, at least fails while daring greatly,
so that his place shall never be with those cold and timid souls
who neither know victory nor defeat."

-Theodore Roosevelt

DECIDING ON ALTRUISM

> *The human race was created to be heroes.*

The world is full of inspiring examples of heroism and selflessness. Gandhi's historic stance against the salt laws when he led the Salt March to Dandi in 1930, igniting the independence movement in India. Rosa Parks' quiet and peaceful refusal to vacate her seat to a white passenger on a segregated bus, effectively launching the Civil Rights Movement. (Following her historic arrest, Ms. Parks went on to live of life of anonymity for many years despite the significant impact she made on equality in America.) The "Chernobyl Three" that knowingly marched to their death when they entered a highly radioactive basement to drain a pool of water forming under the damaged reactor to prevent a second explosion. These were everyday people that performed extraordinary acts for the benefit of humanity, but their reactions were immediate, perhaps instinctive, with any concern for their own personal safety thrust aside for the protection of others. For their own idea of the greater good.

The actions of these selfless individuals have been etched into history. But not every act of courage will be held with the same level of reverence. Some displays of altruistic courage can be found in the thoughts, ideas and motivations of everyday people. Consider public health professionals that toil each day despite limited funding and waning support to protect and improve the health of communities. Or the nonprofit leaders that have dedicated themselves to a life of working with community to promote healthier lifestyles provide assistance and advocate on their behalf despite immense challenges with capacity and fundraising. Or the community organizers that are on the front line, fighting to address deep-rooted systemic issues that continue to entrench disadvantaged and marginalized communities.

Or the social workers, teachers, urban planners, environmental engineers, civic employees, activists, and the list goes on. While each of these careers is as different as the type of individuals that fill them, they likely share two characteristics:

1. They are motivated by a desire to serve.
2. They believe their efforts can change the world.

Moral altruism, known as the ethic of altruism or moralistic altruism, is a doctrine of ethics that holds that moral values associated with one's actions is solely dependent on the impact it has on others, no matter the consequences or the cost it has on the individual themselves.

Studies show the evolutionary origins of genetic traits associated with human cooperation and altruism, but it is the manifestations of the genes that form human thought, resonate feelings, and motivate behavior to ultimately drive us to disregard our own safety, security and gain for the direct benefit of others, to do better by ourselves so that we can do better for others.

There are many problems that afflict our world today. Poverty, hunger, violence, inequality, climate change, governmental corruption, poor educational outcomes, affordable housing and lack of economic opportunity just to name a few. For many of us, awareness of the issues and empathy for those affected by them serves as a catalyst to spur us to action. To do something…anything…to relieve the pain and suffering they cause.

Some of us may join the Peace Corps or go on mission trips to provide aid, dig wells, build houses and schools, or simply demonstrate our compassion for humankind and show that they are not invisible. Others may join nonprofits or start social enterprises that support charitable causes through earned revenue. Still others may dedicate themselves to a career in public or global health, firefighting and EMS, social work, nursing or as a behavioral counselor. Each of these career paths, while unique and very different, all speaks to a sense of displayed selflessness. These types of individuals display behavior characterized by performing acts for others with no apparent benefit to themselves. They believe that the well-being and quality of living of others is just as important than their own comfort and security.

> 'Our awareness and empathy for others is a catalyst for action'

The basic principle of altruism is that man has no right to exist for his own sake, that service to others, to a higher cause, is the only justification for our existence. Indeed, as a society, we often celebrate the selfless acts of others. Individuals that sacrifice their lives for a higher cause, even in war, or firefighters and law enforcement officers that place their lives on the line each day to keep communities safe, or nurses and doctors that sacrifice time away from family and friends to care for the sick and dying.

> *'Service to others, to a higher cause, is the only justification for our existence'*

A book by Matthieu Ricard, "Altruism", supports the idea that by focusing on the well-being of others, we have a potential to save not only our communities, and our society, but also ourselves. Ricard states that by practicing altruism, we can solve some of the world's toughest economic, environmental and sociological problems, which also has a direct individual benefit that leads to longer, healthier and more fulfilled lives. He says "it's what we do every day, giving someone a smile, helping an elderly person, taking underprivileged kids on an afternoon holiday, it's not so difficult...there is always good woven into the fabric in our lives and we must pay more attention to that and also be a part of it."

This seems so simple, but the trick is that you have to believe it in your heart, mind and soul. Being mindful alone is not enough to effect societal change and manifest an altruistic society. We have to practice caring mindfulness to create change within ourselves so that the very best, most powerful version of ourselves has the confidence, self-awareness, compassion and humility to work in partnership and, through your positive example, lead others towards greater change in the world.

If you are looking for some practical, actional advice, ethics professor Julian Savulescu from Oxford University, and Walter Sinnott-Armstrong, of Duke University, provide simple examples of how one may become an effective altruist:

1. **Don't support useless or harmful causes.** A central tenet of altruism is to not harm or create waste. Exploring many newspaper headlines, we can see examples of where many companies, including charities and nonprofits, have been self-serving and corrupt. But for every one of these cases, there are a number of organizations that are truly

doing good and they survive on the efforts of well-intended volunteers. We all have different sets of skills, experiences, backgrounds and expertise that are valuable to these causes, and add to the rich diversity that advances their benefits.

2. **Do what you enjoy and excel at it.** This seems a simple concept, yet so many people donate not because they are compelled to, but because they feel pressured or obligated to. This lackluster commitment lends to being demotivated in giving and may mean that they don't donate, or commit, to the same level as they would if they were genuinely inspired to. If you don't particularly feel connected to animals, then a humane society may not be the best place to volunteer or give to. Likewise, if you are entirely interested in space or science, then supporting the Carnegie Institution for Science probably won't be worthwhile to you. Follow what is personally inspiring to you and find causes that can benefit from your passion.

3. **Spread the love.** Truly one person cannot change the world, but one person can inspire the actions of many. When you discover the passion that ignites

your efforts, you may feel naturally inclined to seek the support and collaborative efforts of your friends, family and colleagues to join in the effort, after all, many hands make light work. Even if you encounter people that are equally passionate about giving back, but don't share your passion, encourage them to follow their path. Be the seed that germinates the field of possibilities.

4. **Use carrots rather than sticks.** Offer praise and accolades to those that are doing more than their fair share of good in the world. Conversely, criticizing does little to uplift or improve people's efforts; in fact, it actually deflates the potential to do more, and may well discourage the emerging do-gooder from becoming involved. Offering praise and recognition increases contributions and advances altruistic efforts.

5. **Avoid overconfidence.** The world is an uncertain place and it is hard to determine what the future will hold. Who would have thought after the Affordable Care Act was enacted in 2013 that the

United States would be faced with an entire healthcare facelift only six years later? Humility is essential when faced with the unknown and uncertain. Saint Augustine once said that it is "pride that changed angels into devils; it is humility that makes men as angels." Augustine was, of course, referencing Lucifer's famous declaration in the Bible, "I will not serve" when he rejected God and descended from his place in Heaven. If to not serve is to liken us to a dubious character such as Satan, then the most honorable and virtuous option is to serve others so that we may endeavor to be like angels. Humility is not an exclusively religious virtue, though it stands to reason that many of societies ideals stem from lessons found in religious texts. Service to others, and to a cause greater than self, requires humility and selflessness, and those are virtues that bear real fruit.

Identifying these personal attributes and virtues within ourselves allows us to better understand what is truly important to us, personally and deeply, and to determine what causes we can best impact through our time, talents, and treasures. It is in the interconnectedness of these gifts that we foster our strongest sense of stewardship to find our purpose.

FINDING YOUR PURPOSE

"He who has a 'why' to live can bear almost any how."

-Friedrich Nietzsche

In a commencement speech at Harvard University, Mark Zuckerberg, the co-founder of Facebook, said, "Purpose is the sense that we are part of something bigger than ourselves. That we are needed, that we have something better ahead to work for. Purpose is what creates true happiness." What is important to understand from this speech is that true happiness can only be found when in service to something greater than yourself, when in service to others. Whether it is your family, your significant other, in service to your communities or if it is in more altruistic causes like bringing clean drinking water to underdeveloped countries, helping the persecuted escape injustice, our providing support to those dealing with depression, it is through your own purpose that you will be genuinely fulfilled.

Our purpose is typically an unconscious, yet underlying current, that shapes the microcosm of our lives. The little decisions and choices we make in our lives; what we eat, what we wear, where we go, who we choose as friends are all indicative, even in their small way, of what is important to our identity as a person. They are what gives us a sense of who we are. If you want to understand your purpose, ask yourself *why* you do what you do. We become so accustomed to daily routines, rituals, and habits, that we rarely stop to ask this simple but crucial question. What values are at the core of your day to day behavior?

Once you identify your "why" and understand its value to your happiness and self-fulfillment, you will begin to move forward with greater speed, energy and intention because you will recognize that your purpose depends on it. Your purpose depends on your efforts, thoughts, ideas, and actions today to bring about what you desire and dream for tomorrow. In many cases, this is an uphill battle rife with challenges, barriers and setbacks. It will require determination, unbending resolve, and a toughness that can only be defined and advanced by the values that support your purpose.

If you truly wish to succeed in your work, to reach your goals, you must find your purpose for pursuing those goals. For the highly actualized individual, purpose is the guiding principle behind thoughts, words, and actions. Many people seek out their purpose, as if it has been lost, as if it is some ancient relic to discover. They believe that to find this purpose, all the secrets of the cosmos will be revealed to them and they will suddenly understand why they are here and what they were meant to do. But purpose is not something that resides externally and waiting to be discovered, it is something that lives within you.

Although your purpose has likely always been there sometimes it can be buried under layers of familial expectations, self-perceptions and societal norms. It has been waiting patiently to reveal itself. Your purpose is in your heart and in your passions, igniting your interests and desires. It is waiting for you to become present in the moment and acknowledge the abundance that surrounds you.

> *'Your purpose depends on your efforts, thoughts, ideas, and actions today to bring about change tomorrow'*

Becoming present means allowing the stresses, anxieties, worries, and self-deprecating thoughts that consume your mind and inhibit your success to dissolve and disappear so the path in front of you can be revealed. As the path becomes clear, one moment will lead you to the next, and the next, and the next, until you begin to live fully in the present, unconcerned with the failures of yesterday or the uncertainties of tomorrow,

You will focus completely on what you are able to do today.

Dr. Nicholas Pearce, Kellogg School of Management professor and pastor at Chicago's Apostolic Church of God, designed a guide to assist people in identifying and pursuing their authentic life's work. In his book *The Purpose Path*, Dr. Pearce presents a bold, new concept called *vocational* courage that guides us to build a life of significance, and outlines five key questions we can consider to determine and align our purpose with what we do, and begin to pursue our life's work.

1. What is success?
2. Who am I?
3. Why am I here?
4. Am I running the right race?
5. Am I running the race well?

Taking the time to ponder and consider these questions allows an opportunity to reflect on the thoughts and ideas they form in your mind, understand the strength and benefit of your experiences, and acknowledge the feelings that resonate within your soul. Through these invocations, you can begin to gain clarity and direction to more intentionally pursue your purpose.

My own experiences in the military, being deployed to combat areas, and as a professional firefighter have helped to develop the "hard crust" of mental toughness, but the ability to develop resiliency outside of these unique environments can also be found in the lessons of the Stoics. Stoicism teaches the power of perception and how we use our own perception of events in our lives to determine how they affect us. Marcus Aurelius, Roman Emperor and famous Stoic philosopher, wrote "choose not to be harmed and you won't feel harmed. Don't feel harmed and you haven't been." It places the power to be affected by something, good, bad or indifferent, directly within our own realm of control. When you develop this mental toughness, then you can begin to align your actions with your purpose, and you will have the power to create solutions out of seemingly hopeless situations, to solve the unsolvable, defeat the undefeatable, overcome the insurmountable, and realize the impossible.

Finding your purpose and having the courage to follow it allows you to live a life of integrity. Recognizing and understanding your purpose provides the assurance of knowing who you are, what you are about, what is important to you and why you exist. Only when you know yourself can you begin to help others. I have always known that my purpose, what I have been called to do, is in service to others. From joining the military and serving around the world on humanitarian and peace-keeping missions, to serving the community as a professional firefighter. When a back injury caused me to leave the fire service after 15 years, I decided to go into healthcare, and eventually public health to help communities achieve the opportunity to reach their highest potential of health and well-being. While the career paths have been starkly different, the underlying theme has always been serving others.

Establishing your purpose as your true north or guiding star also means adopting a unique set of principles that support your decisions, guide your goals, and define your thoughts and ideas. You may begin to have a lucid understanding of your direction, objectives, and actions and find comfort in the transparency this elicits. However, if you fail to discover your purpose, you choose to remain fragmented and unaware of your calling. When you ignore your inner voice, the pit in your stomach and the ache in your heart, you choose to be "just" content rather than truly happy. You may find comfort rather than achievement, you may pacify your desired aims or prosperity with things that offer no meaningful fulfillment, and you may choose, rather, to live a life dwelling on the failures of the past or dreaming for miracles to occur. You may miss the moments that occur in the present that will reveal opportunities for your future, and you may continue to stumble down an unknown path that may lead to virtually nowhere. You may miss your opportunity for greatness.

If you choose, however, to be fulfilled, to be satisfied, and to pursue opportunities that allow you live alongside your passions, you are positioning yourself to live a life of purpose. If you have not yet determined what that may be, the following list from Jack Canfield may help you discover what is meaningful and important to you:

>What do you love to do?
>
>What is something that comes easily to you? (Playing an instrument, singing, writing, sports, etc.)
>
>What are two qualities that you most enjoy expressing in the world?
>
>What are two ways you most enjoy expressing these qualities?

Create a statement that would describe your ideal view of the world if it were perfect in your eyes. This will be your life purpose statement.

>Where are you now in your life or work?
>
>Where do you wish you could be?
>
>If your life were perfect, what would it look like?
>
>What would you be doing with your life?

Another tool that you can use to discover your passions is a simple assessment created by Janet and Chris Attwood called 'The Passion Test'. All you do is fill in the blank for the following question and repeat it until you have come up with fifteen ideal aspects that make your life complete.

My life is ideal when I'm _____

After you have completed 15 different items or statements, you select the top five by comparing 1 to 2, deciding which is more important, and then comparing that one to the third item, and so forth until you have compared all 15 statements. Then you repeat the process until you determined your top 5 passions. Finally, you put these five passions into one sentence and add measurable indicators. An example might be:

"When I am helping communities work with systems to create healthier and happier places to live, I am working with 20 coalitions across 5 counties that represent more than 5 million people, and each coalition

is making measurable and sustainable progress in areas of affordable housing, chronic disease prevention, mental health, homelessness, and climate change."

Once you have completed this step, you can begin to put action plans in place to pursue these goals. Use the tool on the following pages to discover your own passions and take the first step towards finding your purpose.

Passion Statements

My life is ideal when I'm _____

My life is ideal when I'm _____

My life is ideal when I'm _____

My life is ideal when I'm _____

My life is ideal when I'm _____

My life is ideal when I'm _____

My life is ideal when I'm _____

My life is ideal when I'm _____

My life is ideal when I'm _____

My life is ideal when I'm _____

My life is ideal when I'm _____

My life is ideal when I'm _____

My life is ideal when I'm _____

My life is ideal when I'm _____

My life is ideal when I'm _____

My Top Five Passions

#1 _____

#2 _____

#3 _____

#4 _____

#5 _____

Once you know why you do what you do, you will gradually start to bring intention to every action. This process may take time, and it may happen in an instant. When you understand your personal 'why'; the collective reasons that you do what you do, you are ready to start creating a vision for who you want to be; for yourself, your family, and your community.

CREATING YOUR VISION

Vision without action is merely a dream.

Action without vision just passes the time.

Vision with action can change the world

- Joel A. Barker

At this point, you have may committed to altruism and taken steps to define your purpose in life. You know what you want to do, or be a part of, or affect, but do you know how you will advance towards your purpose?

Your vision determines your destination. When you decide where you want to be in your life and when you wish to arrive, you need to plot your course to reach it and consider all the variables, obstacles, and "traffic" you may encounter along the journey.

Stop and ask yourself, where do you want to be in your life in the next ten years? In the next five years?

Next year?
Next month?
Next week?
Tomorrow?

The answer to these questions depends on the vision you have for yourself and what you wish to achieve in your life. It depends on where you are developmentally or professionally, how clearly you are focused on your goals, how determined you are to reach them, and what kind of person you are willing to become to make your dream a reality.

> *'Your vision depends on how clearly you are focused on your goals, how determined you are to reach them, and what kind of person you are willing to become to make your dream a reality'*

Vision is not something that you can estimate or approximate, it is not something tangible that can be held in your hands or seen with your eyes. Vision can be seen through your mind's eye and felt in your heart when you think about your dreams and all that you wish to accomplish. The impacts of your vision may be tangible, however, your vision itself is as invisible as the air you breathe. Just because you cannot see the air, or the microscopic molecules that make up its chemical structure, does not mean it is not there, that you are not able to breath, to fill your lungs with the cool, life-giving element that gives you function and sustains your life. When you establish your vision, the pursuit of it becomes somewhat second nature, a subconscious motivation that directs your thoughts and drives your actions. You don't have to think about breathing in order to draw a breath, nor do you have to concentrate on making your heart pump blood in order for it to beat. It just beats. Your vision provides you the picture in your mind of who you are, where you are going, and what you want to achieve. When spoken, it paints a picture of your idea for the future and the endless possibilities that may come from it. Power comes when you understand that you are the co-creator of your destiny. Whatever you wish to achieve in life, you can manifest through thought, concentration or prayer. This does not mean that all you have to do is think it into existence and, poof, it appears, but rather based on your thoughts, your abilities, your determination and actions, you are capable of achieving whatever vision you are willing to work for. You must take ownership of your vision and make it so massive, so great, and so amazing that it makes you uncomfortable to imagine your life without it. A proven way to fulfill your purpose in life is to visualize achieving that purpose to create your path forward and then take the first step towards actualizing it into existence.

So, what is *your* vision? Painting that picture is the single most important thing you can do to begin creating change within yourself and establishing your future. Having a clear understanding of the results you aim to achieve is what will inspire you to act. It will create the energy you need to take that first step. Consider the *following as a way to develop your vision.*

It should inspire action

It should guide your goals, objectives, and decisions

It should be clear and focused

It should be positive and personally motivating

It should be big enough to encourage and inspire

It should change thoughts, attitudes, and perceptions

It should be heart-driven

When your vision includes others, the impact of your energy has the potential to create ripples across others and, like a current, carry them forward as well. This movement is the power of your vision inspiring action. As a change leader, having a strong and powerful vision is like a magnet, drawing ideas, inspiring people and attracting resources. It creates the energy necessary for change to occur and unifies others under a shared sense of purpose and goals. As a change leader, one of your greatest responsibilities must be to think about what shared vision and purpose exists in your community, and what it will take to motivate people to action. Consider asking yourself the following questions.

What is my vision for change?

Who is affected by the change and how can they be involved in creating that change?

Does it reflect everything you want? Everything they want or need?

How can I inspire them to take action to affect this change?

The process of committing to altruism, defining a sense of purpose, and establishing a vision is the process of creating intention in your life. You are taking deliberate steps in becoming a better person and (indirectly) inspiring others to think about doing the same. In the next section, we will discuss how to implement your plans in simple, actionable steps, because at the end of the day, we are what we *do*, not what we say we'll do.

INTENTIONAL ACTION

BE INTENTIONAL

"A glint of intention initiates the process of creation"

- *Debasish Mridha*

Being intentional means being purposeful in your words and actions. It means choosing to operate according to a set of values and beliefs that are meaningful and fulfilling to you. By being intentional, you have chosen to be an active participant in your life, engaging with yourself and others in a way that brings increased value to each day. It means living simply, or simply living, despite the noise, chaos and hectic pace of life rushing by. When you choose to live a life guided by your purpose, and you are intentional in your thoughts, words, and actions to ensure they are in pursuit of that purpose, you may begin to reject the distractions of popular culture zeitgeist that can lead you away from your path or place in circumstances that are contrary to your purpose. Intentionality can bring clarity, order and serenity to your life if you allow it. When you awake with intention, one of your first thoughts might be how you will make today greater than, and more successful, than yesterday. It means that you look at challenges as opportunities to learn, grow, and improve. And because you can see your own confidence and power as you boldly confront your challenges.

Intention provides a unique sense of connection to the universe, to our Creator. Deepak Chopra calls intention a "force of nature…that creates our reality." It is about bringing fulfillment into your life and allowing it to orchestrate your dreams. When you are intentional, you may begin to understand the infinite power of organization and design at your disposal. In fact, in order to manifest your vision into reality, all that is needed is to visualize the intended outcomes and activate the steps to reach those goals. Being intentional in your thoughts, words, and actions allows you to break the false sense of dependency you have with crutches in your life and listen for the answers that come from within. Crutches are tools that we all need from time to time in our lives to lean on when we are tired, to rely on when we are injured, and to aid us when we need to heal. But the danger lies when we begin to rely on the crutch and believe it is necessary to operate or to survive. Crutches can come in the form of a belief that you lack ability because you were once knocked down. It may be a habit you developed that preoccupies your thoughts and consumes your actions. It may be a lack of confidence or a loss of hope in others. But when you live intentionally, you can begin to recognize when you develop them, and welcome the challenges they present because of the lessons they teach. You can begin to live with less anxiety because there is nothing that can take away your ability to control how you feel, or how you allow things to affect you. Practicing intentionality brings fresh perspectives to old problems. You can be more responsive to unexpected issues or challenges rather than reacting to them. You may learn to listen to fear rather than cower from it, welcoming the opportunity to persevere and overcome its voice of desperation and doubt. You accept that change happens rather than resist it, and you can encourage and lead others to bravely embrace possibilities that it can bring.

Living with intention permits you the ability to feel the need to do more than just maintain or survive. You are intentional because you are able to dream, to picture clearly in your mind what your life should look like and how the world can be. You practice intention because you aspire to more, and you inspire more in others. Intentionality is not only for spiritual gurus or highly enlightened ones; everyone can learn to live an intentional life and, while it is not difficult, it requires laying a strong foundation.

> *'Your choices define you'*

Each day, you are presented with opportunities to make decisions on how you are going to approach the day's tasks, how you are going to interact with people and how you are going to allow those people and tasks to affect you. Each new day is a fresh opportunity to be more focused, more inspired, or more authentic than the day before, to be more in aware of how you feel and better able to navigate emotions, to be more powerful and resolute in your actions and the impact others have on you, and you have on the world around you.

> *'Your environment directs you'*

We find ourselves in many different types of cultures each day from the culture we have established in our home, in our workplace, and within the relationships we have with friends and colleagues. Culture is not static or inanimate. It is a living, breathing force that flows through you and around you, and when you live intentionally, it is important to acknowledge its power and determine if you will allow it to consume you or how you choose to allow it to define and affect you.

> 'What makes you special is within you'

To truly live with intention, you need to look within yourself and recognize what makes you unique is your passions, knowledge, talents, skills, experiences, and even your flaws, scars and vulnerabilities. Each of these characteristics is like individual threads, fragile, delicate and seemingly powerless by themselves, but when woven together, make up the fabric of our being. When you pull on each thread, you can see how it connects and intertwines with the other parts of you, giving you depth and structure, and strengthening your character. When you understand and appreciate the beauty and complexity in your own design, you can begin to use the power of intentionality to live your purpose each day with every thought, word and action.

> *'Doing all things with intention gives you a real opportunity to live a life of meaning, purpose and value for yourself and for others.'*

In order to prepare yourself to achieve intention in your life, you may want to consider the following questions:

Who am I?
What is important to me?
Who are the people that bring light to my life?
What am I passionate about?
Am I aware of the choices I make in each moment of my day?
Do I focus on what is important?
Do I recognize and celebrate my imperfections?
How do I use my imperfections as strengths?
Am I forgiving?
Do I live in the present moment?
Do I compare myself to others or do I live my own life?
Do I enjoy each moment of my life?

> *'Everywhere you look is an opportunity to learn, receive, and understand'*

Putting it into Practice. To begin to live intentionally, it's important to adopt practical steps in order to create new habits. When you incorporate these steps into your life, you will notice that you will have far less stress, anxiety, and feel less pressure to appease others. When you stop trying to be the person that you think others want you to be, you can begin to live a life that is personally satisfying, and only then can you really understand the value of being in service to others as a vehicle to self fulfillment. Determine what you want to contribute to in your life and how you would like that to be communicated. Identify the good that lies within you that is greater than the sum of all your parts and decide what type of impact you will make by channeling that good towards a need or cause. Set your goals to reaching that purpose and stick to them. Allow them to define your thoughts, actions, intentions and motivations. This is the single most important step to bring intentionality into your life. Mitigate the distractions and the noise of the world, and the critics that think they know you better than you do. These distractions will always exist, and it is impossible to shut them all out or to avoid being wounded by them, but when we are aware of them and can anticipate them, we can limit the value and impact they have on us.

Make it a point to put down the smartphone, shut off the television, and close your laptop. Breath in the peace and quiet of inner solitude. Listen to your heart and allow it to shape your moment and set the tone for your day. Listen with intent and learn from the things around you. Everywhere you look is an opportunity to learn, receive and understand. It may come from nature, from your relationships, in your work, or in your observations of the world. Learning from watching allows you to take the good along with the bad. It is in this humility and openness that you can learn as much from success and accomplishments as you can from mistakes and missteps.

CHARACTER IS WHO YOU ARE

"Be more concerned with your character than your reputation,

because your character is what you really are,

while your reputation is merely what others think you are."

-John Wooden

French sociologist and philosopher Pierre Bourdieu found that power is created culturally and symbolically through the interplay of agency and structure he coined as 'habitus'. He surmised that habitus guides how we think and behave as the result of society becoming engrained in us through sensibilities, dispositions and taste. In short, habitus is a natural state of being, a way to understand our behavioral traits and why we act in some of the ways we do.

Character on the other hand, is taking the natural reactions of habitus and applying them to action. It is the value, energy, and service that we put into a particular circumstance. When we understand what values are important to us, and we remain loyal to that moral code, we begin to develop a moral character that is defined by who we are and how we are perceived by others. Your character is so much more than your reputation. Character is who you really are under the facade you have created to present to society; beneath the political correctness and pleasantries you institute in order to remain blissfully neutral in a controversial world. Your character includes a variety of attributes, including the existence or lack of qualities such as empathy, honesty, responsibility, accountability, loyalty, or courage. These are omnipresent within you; they define you and are constantly there even when no one is watching. Abraham Lincoln famously said, "Character is like a tree and reputation like its shadow. The shadow is what we think of it; the tree is the real thing." Too often, we see the shadow of people and project that image to be the representation of who they are on the inside.

When I was in graduate school, I had a chance to hear a guest speaker talk about the need to make transformational changes in the health care system to improve the lives of disadvantaged communities. I was inspired by this individual and held them in admiration, even awe. Several years later, I had an opportunity to work with them on various occasions and, through several unfortunate experiences, I discovered that their true character was one of pretense, deceit and hypocrisy. This was a disturbing, hurtful, but powerful lesson for me as it created an enormous shift in my awareness of the power of our character. Many times, we do not discover the truth until it is too late, if ever revealed at all. Conversely, your own character may be defined by the perceptions of others based on your reputation or their interactions with you, even if limited. Sometimes, the reputation you have with a few people is how others within their network portray you, even if you have never directly interacted with them. Reputation is important because of the perception it creates within the opinions and views of others, but it is your character that defines you.

The term 'character' is in and of itself morally neutral. This means that everyone from the Pope to the tyrants of history have a list of character traits unique to them, and, while some may be starkly different, you may be surprised to find that many are the same. Your character determines how you really think and feel about things you see, hear and experience. For instance, what is your initial thought, feeling or instinctual reaction to the following situations?

When you see someone that is experiencing homelessness.

When you drive by a group of day workers gathering on a corner.

When you are behind someone in the grocery store separating items on the conveyor and using various forms of assistance to buy basic food items.

When you observe two people of the same gender holding hands affectionately strolling through the mall.

When you watch the news and see children of migrants being locked up in holding facilities, being denied basic necessities of life.

> 'Your character, who you really are inside, determines how you will respond to certain events, situations, and circumstances in your life.'

As a society, we have a list of rules we have established informally and over time that defines certain behavior as socially acceptable, or conversely, reprehensible, and the more prominent character traits that are displayed is how we distinguish individuals with "good" character from those of questionable or "bad" character. As a society, we love to put labels on things and people. In many ways, labels are necessary for survival. For instance, if we did not label things that are 'hot', they may burn us, and if we do not refer to things as 'dangerous', we may be injured or maimed by them. However, labels are not always necessary and can often increase the divide that exists between groups and classes. Rich versus poor; high class versus low class; good versus bad; nice versus mean; handsome versus ugly; educated versus uneducated; white versus black. And despite the list of labels being seemingly endless, we have a loose method of assigning these categories. We may label someone "good" because we determine their general nature to show responsibility, loyalty and kindness. But this practice is somewhat superficial because character is not defined by a person's good intentions or through a single interaction. Character is defined by your unwavering commitment to live by a personal set of moral values and to practice those values each day with every action you take. This means that you choose to be guided by a personal set of principles despite the consequences of those actions, or the challenges you may face as a result of the commitment you have made to live by your personal ethos.

Strong character is what is needed to transform practices, change paradigms and shift power dynamics in order to pursue justice, stand for what you believe is right, speak for the voiceless, act for the fearful, honor the memory of the fallen and seek more equitable outcomes for the neglected and ignored.

But what are the character traits necessary to possess in order to create change within the world? While integrity, honesty and compassion are obvious choices, and certainly admirable traits in any person regardless of whom you are or what you hope to achieve, there are other traits that we can adopt within ourselves so that we are adequately prepared to create change in the world. These character traits may include flexibility, responsibility, ambition, creativity, confidence, being a problem solver, open-minded, results-oriented, and open to strong, positive dialogue.

"The measure of intelligence is the ability to change."

-Albert Einstein

Flexibility. Successful agents of change are flexible and must be in order to adjust, not only to the change they seek to effect, but also to the shifting dynamics within their team, culture or environment. Striving for transformative change can mean having a lack of control over circumstances or factors that impact your work, but only you can control how you will respond to those factors. As a successful change maker, growing your ability to be in tune and receptive in order to anticipate changes, being nimble and ready to respond and pivot when needed, and above all else, refusing to be paralyzed by the unexpected is essential to continue to drive forward towards completion. This means that we must begin to shift our mindsets to view adversity, and the anxiety and uncertainty it brings, as a nourishing opportunity for growth and development. Being flexible to the changing environment and circumstances offers lessons that may improve our life, change our perspectives, or give us direction in the future. Viewing adversity in this light, however, means that we may be faced with tough choices and decisions to how we allow adversity to affect us, and how much effort we want to give to those moments.

"A hero is someone who understands the responsibility that comes with his freedom."

-Bob Dylan

Responsibility. Being responsible means being accountable for the impact of your thoughts, words and actions. It requires having a clear understanding of the expectations of your role in the group, as a leader, or to your community and working diligently to fulfill those obligations. Change agents use self-control, are thoughtful in how they respond and respect the feelings and needs of others. Change agents also recognize when they have competing interests and use sound judgment and discernment to be strong stewards of the greater good, regardless of how they may personally feel. This may be particularly difficult for the policy maker or elected official when the greater good means acting in a way that serves the interests and needs of the greater population, even when it is in conflict with the ideals of their base. I'm less certain if that should require legislators and politicians be change makers, after all, isn't the role of a public servant to serve the whole public? Should their role be to bend the public to their will, or is it the privilege of their positions to bend to the will of the People? Change agents are effective team players and emerge as strong collaborators committed to collective success. Above all, they strive to put their best efforts forward; they honor the commitments they have made to themselves, their communities, or their constituents, meeting their deadlines, owning up to their mistakes and admitting when they are wrong.

"Both tears and sweat are salty, but they render a different result. Tears will get you sympathy; sweat will get you change."

-Jesse Jackson

Results-oriented. Change agents are outcome-focused and understand that all their efforts are in vain if they do not lead to positively impacting the cause behind their efforts. This means transitioning from providing a service to delivering results that are show measurable improvement and sustainability. An example might be providing donated winter coats to people that are experiencing homelessness. While a valiant and important cause, being result-oriented might include working with other organizations that serve the population to ensure mass distribution, ensure a coat is put directly into the hands of the people that need them, and that the effort can be tracked to measure an improvement in distribution and receipt, a reduction in number needed, or an improvement in cold-related illnesses and/or deaths. Another option may be to focus equal or greater energy on social improvement strategies such as affordable housing, housing-first, or recuperative care initiatives in order to reduce the number of individuals that even need basic necessities.

Results-oriented changemakers are consciously aware of the importance and consideration of the details, but do not allow, "getting into the weeds" to be an impedance to progress. Less time is associated with a specific process so that the most effective or valuable methods can be applied. Change makers maintain a steadfast focus on achieving goals and objectives that lead to impact and, as a result, only put the required time and energy necessary into tasks and activities that lead to those desired results. Results-oriented change agents have the ability to "think big", to look beyond what is immediate and focus clearly on what lies ahead. The following tools may help you develop skills necessary to ensure your efforts are focused on results.

1. Set clear goals
2. Provide resources and tools
3. Improve dialogue and open communication
4. Invest in praise and self-gratitude
5. Be actionable

"Great ambition is the passion of a great character. Those endowed with it may perform very good or very bad acts. All depends on the principles which direct them."

-Napoleon Bonaparte

Ambitious. Having a passion for results, effective change makers have no problem rolling up their sleeves to dig into the work. They set ambitious and lofty goals and are willing to put in the hours, to over-promise *and* over-deliver, to assume a leadership role and carry the team in order to achieve outcomes. They have a unique ability and strength to control the forces of ambition and mold them to work in alignment with their own goals and objectives. Change makers understand that in order to achieve big results, they must be willing to take risks and accept failures as only temporary setbacks and opportunities to learn. Most importantly, in order to pursue ambitious goals, change makers must surround themselves with other ambitious people. Jim Rohn said: "You are the average of the five people you spend the most time with", but the reality is you are the average of all the people in your network. While there is value in paying attention to criticism and objection, allowing doubters, critics and naysayers to impede your progress will not get you anywhere, but surrounding yourself with other ambitious, bold and fearless leaders can propel you towards the change you desire.

"Creativity is inventing, experimenting, growing, taking risks, breaking rules, making mistakes, and having fun."

-Mary Lou Cook

Creativity. Creativity is one of the most important attributes of the modern leader. They have the courage and tenacity to abandon the safety of "group think" and seek out new ways of doing things. By looking at ideas and problems with open perspective, they discover innovative solutions to complex issues. They have the ability to think outside of the box by understanding how the box is designed and what is already in it. Effective change agents ask questions, challenge conventional thought, and refuse to maintain status quo out of comfort or fear. They embrace change as an exciting opportunity to continue to grow, learn and solve problems. Elon Musk is an obvious and powerful influencer for creative change leadership. All of his innovative efforts have been central to a vision to improve humanity either through automation and automobiles powered by renewable energy, reducing global warming through solar power expansion, or exploring space colonization as an effort to prevent human extinction. Professor Wangari Maathai, founder of the Green Belt Movement, a grass-roots organization that battled poverty and environmental protection through tree planting. A Nobel Peace Prize laureate, as well, she was internationally acclaimed for her efforts to improve democracy, human rights, and environmental conservation.

"Optimism is the faith that leads to achievement. Nothing can be done without hope and confidence."

-Helen Keller

Confidence. One of the most significant and influential motivators of behavior is a person's self-confidence. Studies have shown that how someone perceives their own capabilities and self-worth directly affects their ability to achieve success. Self-confidence is not something we are born with, it is a learned behavior, but it is also mindset that requires constant reinforcement through positive thinking, practice, and talking with others to understand, and acknowledge, the value you hold and what you have to offer others. Confidence comes from your own internal feeling of well being, self-esteem, and belief in your ability to thrive. Change agents use instinct and intuition as a compass, guiding through the unknown and uncertainty with faith and trust in themselves and the ability of others.

Self-confidence is attributed to two key characteristics: self-efficacy and self-esteem. Self-efficacy can be gained by observing our peers and colleagues developing skills and achieving success through those skills. Self-efficacy mirrors the confidence in our ability to control our thoughts, motivations, behaviors and social interactions, which provide a greater willingness to take on difficult tasks and persevere in the face of adversity. It overlaps self-esteem, which is our ability to see our own worth and recognize our skills and abilities. It as an assurance in ourselves that comes from feeling connected and accepted by the world around us, but it is also rooted in our own beliefs that we are virtuous, capable, and able to accomplish our goals and achieve our dreams.

There is a great tool from Mind Tools that outlines three clear steps for building self-confidence, which mirrors a previously used journey metaphor. The steps are preparing your journey, setting out, and accelerating towards success and can be used to realize your aspirations by building your own self-confidence. You can learn more about this tool by going to mindtools.com/selfconf.

1. **Preparing your journey**
    a. Look at all you have achieved
    b. Think about your strengths
    c. Think about what is important to you and where you want to go
    d. Start managing your mind
    e. Commit yourself to success
2. **Setting Out**
    a. Build the knowledge you need to succeed
    b. Focus on the basics
    c. Set small goals and achieve them
    d. Keep managing your mind
3. **Accelerating towards success**
    a. Keep yourself grounded
    b. Reassess your confidence

Achieving self-confidence starts with thinking positive and affirming thoughts about our skills, abilities and personality, but setting goals and achieving them through consistent action can accelerate it.

"We cannot solve our problems with the same level of thinking that created them."

-Albert Einstein

Problem-solver. The ability to look critically at problems and identify solutions is paramount for those that wish to create positive change in the world. Problem solving requires intuition, logic and emotional intelligence to think instinctively and intelligently. Seek out and seize opportunities to learn and grow intellectually from problems that arise and open your mind to new ways of thinking and analyzing. Change agents that develop an ability to solve problems do not focus on being right or wrong, they are motivated only in the pursuit for what works and what brings hearts and minds together for the greater good. Problem solvers understand that the true value of solving complex issues is in prevention rather than intervention, in preparation versus reaction, and in avoiding conflict instead of creating it. You can focus on solving problems by remaining reasonably objective, while questioning conventional logic.

"A mind is like a parachute. It doesn't work if it is not open."

-Frank Zappa

Open-minded. Being open-minded means having a perpetual thirst for knowledge and a hunger for new experiences. People that create change often describe themselves as lifelong learners. Take every interaction, every experience and every relationship to learn and grow from. Be curious by nature, with a desire to understand the world that surrounds you, to explore and experience it to make better judgments and develop new perspectives. Be cautiously optimistic about the impact your efforts will have and, as a result, be open to considering the perspectives and insights of others. Acknowledge that your own belief system may be limited to your own past experiences and welcome the perspective of others as a way to enrich discussion and present new possibilities. The ability to observe and understand opposing views from different perspectives will allow you to discern, not what is "right" or "wrong", but rather, what "works" and what "does not" work. Part of being open-minded, and leveraging your curiosity, means focusing on the things that "don't work" and trying to understand what about it doesn't work and if there is an opportunity or a change that can be made so that it will work. In the realm of the change agent, absolute thinking is limiting, and possibilities are boundless.

"The most basic of all human needs is the need to understand and be understood. The best way to understand people is to listen to them."

-Ralph G. Nichols

Effective Communication. Communication is a critical component for change initiatives on any scale. It begins when an idea is planted, like a seed, in the minds of those that may be affected, involved, or benefit from the change. Effective change agents must have the ability to inspire and motivate others to take action in pursuit of the cause and use strategic communication to sustain the momentum and energy of the movement. There are a variety of communication mediums that can be used including verbal, written, visual, and non-verbal. They each have an appropriate time and place to be used but they all share the same goal; to transfer information in a way that leads to greater understanding.

"Silence is a lesson learned from the many sufferings of life"

-Seneca, Thyestes, 309

Effective Listening. Effective listening is as important, if not more, than effective communication. Before you can birth an idea, create a plan, and communicate the goal, you must listen to understand the problem. It requires adopting no preconceived opinions or assumptions of the circumstance, maintaining objectivity and open perspective, and asking questions to gain clarity and greater understanding. Too often, people don't truly listen, but rather are waiting to respond. When you listen to truly understand and contemplate, you may identify ideas and solutions from what others say, and sometimes, what they don't say. The fearful and inexperienced are those that talk over others, speak in circles, or ramble on endlessly, in a futile attempt to reassure themselves. Rambling is often a tool used to control people, or to control the narrative. Some do it intentionally so as to not allow others an opportunity to speak. Others ramble due to ego, or because no one has dared to end their self-serving monologue. Still others do it because there is no one they would rather hear speak than themselves. Listening in silence with intention and an open mind is a way to gain personal strength and confidence.

The results you achieve in life are often determined by the way you respond to events or circumstances you face. If it is your character that drives your reactions, then it is your character that will determine your success. Of course, that does not mean that you only need to do "good" in order to be successful, or that those that do "bad" things will not succeed. However, when you choose to do good in the world, when you serve a higher purpose than yourself, and when you live with intention towards that cause, you may develop a different perspective of what success is and you will more likely be fulfilled through your actions.

BE COURAGEOUS

"We can't be afraid of change.

You may feel very secure in the pond that you are in,

but if you never venture out of it,

you will never know that there is such a thing as an ocean, a sea.

Holding onto something that is good for you now,

may be the very reason why you don't have something better."

— C. JoyBell C.

Many have a misguided understanding of what courage is. They believe that it means being fearless, undaunted, and unafraid. The Merriam-Webster dictionary provides a more accurate definition of 'Courage' as "mental or moral strength to venture, persevere, and *withstand* danger, fear, or difficulty." You see, being courageous is not being without fear, but it is about doing what needs to be done in spite of fear. Having the ability to stand your ground and be steadfast in your convictions, unwavering in your beliefs, and undeterred to voice your opinions and share your ideas.

> 'A dream, an idea, a vision are all meaningless without action'

There is no shortage of big thinkers, change makers and visionaries in the world and they swim in a sea of amazing ideas, plans and solutions that have potential to solve the world's biggest problems. They are often captivating, and inspiring with an ability to draw you in by their creative and imaginative ways to help you achieve your dreams. Sadly, most of the time that is all it is…a dream. You see, a dream, an idea, a vision, are meaningless without action. Inaction often comes from a place of fear. Fear of failure. Fear of criticism. Fear of rejection. Fear of making hard decisions. Fear of taking responsibility. Fear of accomplishing results. Fear of being irrelevant. Fear of being wrong. This fear is paralyzing for most, inhibiting their ability to move forward and rendering them powerless to execute; to act.

Many people choose to live in a self-perceived bubble of importance and relevance. There are many names, but some of the more widely used terms that have become common in every industry, and particularly diluted in my opinion, include "visionary", "thought leader", or "guru". By leading others in formulating thoughts and drawing out ideas, they are not responsible for inaction and are protected from scrutiny that may come from ineffectiveness or failure. For many others, the fear of failure is the end. Their fear consumes them, imprisons their ideas, dreams, and beliefs and smothers all opportunities to succeed and achieve. What they do not understand is that fear is the fuel to the fire of triumph. You need courage and persistence to overcome and face your fears, to harness its power and propel you forward.

"Our doubts are traitors, and make us lose the good we oft might win, by fearing to attempt"

-William Shakespeare

Understanding your purpose, having a vision and being intentional are not enough if you are afraid to take the first step. This fear may manifest itself within you in different ways.

Task Trounce. This is where fear may cause you to overthink your problem and solution, to over-analyze the various options, to weigh the costs and benefits of your approach where you look for, and focus, on the challenges, perceived flaws and begin to second guess the effectiveness of your plan. It presents so much doubt in your mind that you may decide to set it aside, to turn your focus to another priority with a plan to revisit your plan later, but you never do. You have talked yourself out of it because you fear the results may not live up to your own expectations.

Perpetual Process. You immerse yourself in the planning and preparation of implementing your dream that you bury yourself in the avalanche of details and nuance. You convince yourself that the plan needs more research, more support, more ideas and facts to substantiate its credibility. You feel safe in this 'design stage' because you have convinced yourself that it is all relevant developmental planning, but the reality is you never allow yourself to prototype and test your concept.

Perfect Paralysis. You refuse to accept any standard short of your own flawless expectations or your perception of other's expectations. You believe that there is only one, divine path forward and you endeavor that each component and every detail will be absolute. Your plan is an "all or nothing approach". You believe that there are wrong ways to do things, and your way is the only right way. Most likely, this behavior is not isolated to one particular dream or concept but is evident in other areas of your life. You have submitted to a life of endless comparison, comparison to other's success, and comparison to your own idea of where you believe you should be. You do not delegate tasks because you do not trust that anyone will be able to execute to the same level as you. You may procrastinate or even avoid situations that you believe you will not excel in or avoid people who you feel intimidated by or that you perceive view you as less than. The cause of your obsession with perfection may vary, but they typically stem from fear, and usually will lead to an inability to execute.

Visionary Syndrome. This type of person can often be counter-productive to progress and success, if not utilized carefully and appropriately. Often times they are enigmatic and possess an ability to inspire and excite friends and colleagues to a plan that is so ambitious in scale and scope, with such an amazing potential for impact that it is nothing short of a miracle that everyone has been dreaming of. Many visionaries have an uncanny ability to sell the dream, displaying a sense of confidence that they have all the pieces to the puzzle and the ability to lead the group to success. They pull coalitions together, ignite passions, and create energy within the group. But when the work is getting started, when the going gets tough, the visionaries get going…right out the door as quickly as possible leaving the invoice on the table. They ride the high of being seen as a visionary, as someone that others look up to, but then often become overwhelmed by the pressure to live up to the character they portray. Much like the great and all-powerful Wizard of Oz, they impress and inspire with shock and awe, but when it comes time to execute the vision, we are left with the man behind the curtain, nothing more than smoke and mirrors.

> '*Fear from anxiety is not real, but the effects of this fear leave lasting scars*'

Each of these characteristics has two underlying themes in common. They are born out of anxiety in the land of fear, and they may well lead to a wasteland of failures and shattered aspirations, where dreams go to die, and opportunities cease to exist. Fear, like success, is hardwired into us all. Just as you were created to succeed and to fulfill a special purpose, you are designed to fear consequences and repercussions. Fear is a natural defense mechanism that prevents you from venturing too close to a ledge, from climbing too high, or sailing too far from the shore. It is an emotional response to an immediate threat that exists within the present moment. Anxiety, however, is a false sense of impending doom. It is your inner voice of doubt and self-sabotage that convinces you that something will go wrong, that you are not good enough, smart enough, accomplished enough, or talented enough to succeed.

Anxiety is like a dense fog that rolls in slowly, blocking your ability to see your path forward, disorienting you and freezing you from movement. Fear from anxiety is not real, but the effects of this fear can leave lasting scars.

Having the courage to silence your anxieties, subside your worries, and face your fears head-on is the only way to lead yourself, and others, in the direction of progress, success and impact. Having courage means you have the confidence to say 'yes' when others say 'no', to persevere when others give up, to embrace and welcome change when others resist, to find ways to make something work when others only find reasons why it cannot, and to run towards success when others withdraw from the race because it is too hard. I have faced many of these same choices in my own life.

While working for a nonprofit organization, I was managing a regional multi-sector coalition to reduce the incidence rate of diabetes in the Inland Empire of

Southern California. After nearly two years into the project, we were making considerable progress despite an ambitious project goal and timeline. However, I began to receive pressure from outside the project, to steer many of the project objectives and goals into a decidedly different direction; one that favored outside interests over the benefit of the community we were charged with serving. With the pressure coming from within my own organization, rather than bend and fold to save my job and livelihood, I chose to remain committed to my principles and maintain the integrity of our cause. I took definitive and intentional steps to block the outside meddling, shield the project members, and address the alleged improprieties within my own organization. Ultimately, I was very unceremoniously terminated, in an effort by the board to contain and conceal what was occurring under their own noses. This, however, is not a lesson in failure, but rather in having the courage to stand for what you believe in and refuse to allow cronyism and corruption to go unchecked. That is not to say that I was not afraid or an emotional wreck during those months. The situation took a heavy toll on my mental health and physical wellbeing, a toll that took more than a year to heal and recover from. But it also provided amazing lessons that I could not have learned if I had made different choices; choices that would not have allowed me to hold my head high and maintain a clear conscience.

Boldly facing your fear of the unknown and marching through the fog of anxiety is a significant way to reach clarity and will reveal what is real versus imagined. This clarity will help you understand that real value is the experience of learning and growing, though not necessarily from success or achievement. Embrace the beauty of imperfection as perfection itself. Striving for a false sense of perfection is like chasing a unicorn. Following my termination, my organization's newly appointed leadership swiftly moved in and attempted to take on my role in the coalition project. Their desire to be seen as an expert, and revered as the "savior", meant that their solution and approach had to be perfect. At the risk of oversimplifying a complex and messy situation, the insecurity that arose from this blind pursuit had a negative impact on the coalition and the initiative was effectively diluted to something far less innovative and transformational from the original intended outcome. When we become too focused on perfection, or our own perception of what perfect looks like, we can quickly lose sight of what is important. Ultimately, we will become disenchanted, frustrated and become less energized in our pursuit. And even though you may become frustrated and frozen in fear, the world continues on without you.

A frustrated person is not someone who is successful or accomplished. A frustrated person is someone who lost sight of their vision and became overwhelmed by fear and indecisiveness. To move forward, you must regain the clarity of your vision, accept that defeat is inevitable, but that it is only temporary. Welcome the opportunity for growth and learning that it presents and walk confidently through the mist to a brighter tomorrow.

STOP TALKING, START ACTING

"Infuse your life with action.

Don't wait for it to happen.

Make it happen.

Make your own future.

Make your own hope.

Make your own love.

And whatever your beliefs, honor your creator,

not by passively waiting for grace to come down from upon high,

but by doing what you can to make grace happen...

yourself, right now,

right down here on Earth."

-Bradley Whitford

Action is defined as "doing something for a particular purpose." In literature, dialogue is an element of the composition that breathes life into the story and its characters, while the narrative is what gives it depth and substance. However, it is action that gives the story motion and carries it along the intended course. Without the action element, the story would be static and stationary with no change or development.

Prior to parting ways from the troubled nonprofit and their impotent board, I had already become disenchanted with their 'profit over purpose' mentality and the autocratic manner in which the organization was being operated. While I was committed to the change initiative I was leading, I knew there was a better way to do collaborative work. I began build out a new type of nonprofit organization that would redefine how sectors and systems collaborate alongside the community with a more intentional focus on advancing equity. Working alongside several colleagues, we visualized what has become *nLab Concepts*, an organization whose mission is *"shifting power dynamics and caring about the greater good"*. This firm, and our driving motivation, is the physical manifestation of our belief that the only way to make sustainable change in society is through collective action and innovative solutions that are led from the very communities they seek to improve. Our collective purpose is spurred forward through the actions and passions of many.

Ludwig von Mises, an Austrian-born economist best known for his work on praxeology (the study of human choice and action), believed that action is a purposeful behavior where people aim to replace "a more satisfactory state of affairs for a less satisfactory." He concluded that for people to be moved to action, three preconditions needed to exist: that they are no longer satisfied with a current condition, that they have a vision for a more desirable alternative, and that they believe they have the power and ability to effect change through action. As in Mises' theory, I was disenchanted with the status quo, had a vision and a belief there was a better way, and somehow found the courage to act on that belief.

Simply stated, change, certainly social change, often happens at the grassroots level. This does not mean that transformational change cannot occur from a more top-down approach, but meaningful and sustainable social change should embody the voice of the community, be inclusive of community leadership, and begin with dialogue and the sharing and acceptance of ideas and beliefs.

For change makers to begin to create change and improve conditions, they must start with dialogue. Not trivial talk or deadpan discussions that portray a false sense of caring or urgency, but genuine conversations that seek to understand the problem. These discussions should aim to discover the root causes and motivations that created and perpetuated the issue, consider various perspectives and viewpoints, and develop a collective vision for how to begin to address the problem. This may seem like an obvious suggestion to some, and a point of pain for others due to the amount of talking and inaction that has occurred for so long. But constructive conversation is necessary to confront the uncomfortable disagreements, differing views and conflicting solutions to break out of the insular bubbles of self-isolation created by silence.

In order to ensure change is meaningful and sustainable, it is critical that change agents work collaboratively with communities, systems and coalitions to find solutions that celebrate diversity, ensure inclusion, and advance opportunities for equity across all races, ethnicities and socioeconomic classes. This means that the walls that have been erected to divide us be broken down so that people can come together as a collective and demand the change they seek with one voice. But how can we, as individuals or community change makers, begin to move from a place of dialogue and understanding to a space where we create actionable and meaningful impact? The answer to this may be in the human-centered design (HCD) approach. Just as the action element is critical to writing a powerful and engaging story, it is woven into the composition through intentional design. HCD is a process that ensures solutions consider the motivations, needs, and values of those impacted by the solution. Though this seems like simple logic, community has long been ignored and left out of decisions that bring programs, services, and resources to their communities. Most of the time, because of the lack of inclusion, the resources are ineffective in their intended purpose because of slow adoption, cultural inappropriateness, or lack of understanding of the true needs of the community. HCD requires an understanding of how individual actions are guided through experiential design in order to achieve widespread social change. The design of effective and meaningful experiences depends on three key principles: inspiration, ideation, and implementation.

> *'Confront uncomfortable disagreements, differing views and conflicting solutions to break out of the insular bubbles of self-isolation created by silence'*

Inspiration. The belief that a person, or community, has the capacity to influence their behavior through their own thoughts and ideas is the definition of agency. This step includes researching, observing, and interacting with people or community in order to immerse yourself and understand their needs, motivations and behaviors. It involves developing empathy and emotional intelligence to better understand their sense of agency and how they interact with potential barriers to the power of agency. A significant part of this process is interviewing individuals and asking questions to better understand the issue and how it motivates their behavior. IDEO, a nonprofit organization that specializes in design thinking, developed a number of valuable tools and resources for those seeking to conduct human-centered design projects. One of these includes the "Five Why's". This is a process by which you will interview an individual by asking why they think or feel a certain way. It requires asking "why" each time a person answers a previous question. While it may seem juvenile or repetitive, IDEO describes it as an excellent way to "uncover deep-rooted motivations and assumptions that underpin a person's behavior." The idea is to begin by asking more broad questions about a person's life, what they value, and what their interests are, before leading into more specific questions that pertain to the issue you are trying to solve. It is important that you record exactly what they say, not your perception of what they mean. You should also pay attention to and take note of both verbal and non-verbal queues. More information on interview tools, methods and resources can be found by visiting IDEO's design kit (www.designkit.org).

Ideation. This step includes identifying themes, patterns and trends from your observations and interactions, and identifying ideas that increase and enhance access to available resources, programs or services. It is important to understand that there is often an abundance of available resources within communities that can be leveraged. Access does not necessarily mean recreating the wheel or designing and developing new programs. Being a change maker means recognizing what already exists and ensuring it is utilized in the most effective and efficient manner for maximum impact. In this stage, you will compile your learning's and research to develop your concept, establish frameworks and design principles, and co-create your solution with collaborators and the community.

Implementation. Finally, in order to achieve impact and advance opportunities for change, you must take action. Implementation of your design is as much about delivering the intended purpose as it is evaluating and gaining feedback from the community. If the design is not achieving the intended outcomes, you must be willing and able to pivot, adapt, and adjust to ensure greater impact. As a change maker, you must have the courage to face your failure, embrace the opportunity to learn from it, and move forward with a better idea. In the end, failure is not determined by how many times you readjust or change; only inaction or inability to find a better way leads to failure. Transformative change in longstanding and complex issues takes time; there is no shortcut to success. Be patient, trust yourself and your team, maintain and encourage ongoing communication with partners and the community, and keep moving forward.

> *'Failure is not determined by how many times you readjust or change, only inaction and inability to find a better way leads to failure.'*

Action requires an understanding of human development and psychology to identify the intrinsic motivations behind why people behave and act in the ways they do. When you understand the motivations behind a person's thoughts and actions, you are able to guide and direct them towards the desired behavior. This same principle can be applied to systems. Recognizing that society lives within the construct of a particular framework, understanding how and why that structure was erected, and working collaboratively to adjust the structure is essential to reform the systems so that they provide benefit for the greater many, rather than the privileged few. To accomplish this, you have to understand and acknowledge the complexity of the systems, as well as the individuals themselves, and how the combination of our collective thoughts, ideas and beliefs created the culture and societies we live in, and by extension, the systems contained within them.

Change makers have to think like innovators. Innovation is key to bringing about impactful change, no matter the scale, scope or context. But what exactly is innovation? There is a great multitude of ways it has been defined, but when they are all distilled, it becomes clear that innovation is the application of an idea that achieves measurable value for a specific problem. Innovation should not be confused with inventing something new. Inventing is the occurrence of a new idea, while innovation is turning that idea into action.

Often times, this means bringing something that has worked in one market and applying to a different market for a different purpose to achieve a different result. An example of this differentiation is in touchscreen technology. Many may be surprised to discover that touchscreen tech was developed in the early 1980's for cameras to be able to create finger drawings. It was not until Apple applied the technology to the emerging iPhone that the multitouch screen technology had a greater marketable purpose. The technology was the invention and the application to the iPhone was the innovation.

> 'Innovation is taking something that has worked in another market, and applying to a different market, for a different purpose to achieve a different result'

Similarly, healthcare innovations are changing the way primary care physicians monitor patient adherence to medications and care plans. For example, patients being treated for diabetes with the lowest levels of compliance to medication regimes have a 17% higher annual risk for hospitalization than diabetic patients with greater compliance. With an estimated 1 trillion connected devices expected to sell by the year 2020, wearable devices offer an opportunity to increase patient engagement, improve compliance, and enhance prevention strategies. The health care innovation space has erupted in recent years with a number of new enterprises focused on providing the support, resources and funding opportunities for innovative solutions. One of these new enterprises is TreeHouse Health, an innovation hub based in Minneapolis, that serves as a nontraditional incubator and accelerator focused on advancing "innovation in healthcare by investing and partnering with emerging companies." Since 2013, TreeHouse has worked with more than 15 companies from various sectors of healthcare including health IT, devices, and diagnostics, providing early stage investment and long-term support and growth. Another innovator in the healthcare space is ScaleLA, an incubator that has connected innovation, multi-sector collaboration, and community to support startups, inspire progressive leadership, and engage community. Through their creative model, they are leveraging the talent and entrepreneurial spirit that exists in their community to solve some of the most complex systemic challenges their region faces and using the power of government to put those ideas into action.

> *'It takes definitive action to bring meaningful value to an idea'*

Public health, a sector that has traditionally focused on protecting the public from the spread of disease, has arguably been in a more defensive stance, reacting to epidemics as they arise. Over the past 150 years, however, public health began linking the science of intervention development and implementation with efforts to increase public understanding, adherence and social commitment to improving health. Today, public health agencies are forming multi sector collaborations with partners from healthcare, social sector, and municipal governments to focus on health equity, and racial and social justice issues because of the direct connection they have identified between housing, public safety, food access, behavioral health in schools, and quality jobs as social determinants of health. The incorporation of nontraditional partners and focus on social issues, and the structural drivers that cause them, are considered innovations in public and population health strategies. All of these examples, while different in issue and approach, show that it takes action to bring meaningful value to an idea. A number of investigators have been studying business over the last several decades to better understand how creativity drives innovation. *'Managing Change, Creativity & Innovation'*, a book written by Patrick Dawson and Costas Andriopoulos based on their own research, found that when change initiatives are approached through a human and social process, rather than a systems approach, yields greater results in driving creativity and innovation towards change. Warren Bennis, professor of organizational leadership and advisor to four U.S. Presidents, brought together a collection of case studies in his book, *'Organizing Genius: The Secrets of Creative Collaboration'*, of several extraordinary groups that drove change by harnessing creative collaboration.

Yet, despite the overwhelming research that finds unlocking creative potential is the driver to economic growth, and that companies that harness creativity almost always outperform their competitors and peers, public health seems to be lacking in the use of innovation and creativity. A report written by the de Beaumont Foundation, based on the Public Health Interests and Needs Survey (PH WINS) released in June 2019, found that "only 43% of respondents say creativity and innovation are rewarded in their organization." The report offers suggestions on how public health leaders can commit to fostering environments that allow innovation, creativity and the freedom to experiment, solve problems and cross-collaborate within the organization to learn, ideate and grow.

> *'Talk is cheap, but action cannot be ignored'*

Understanding what action is and how design thinking can help to develop deeper understanding and arrive at concepts is critical to ensuring the change you are attempting to create is necessary, relevant and meaningful to the community it is for, and sustainable in the long-term. Just as understanding the importance of an action element in a storyline, the process by which that action element is designed is also helpful. Telling a good action story is about setting the right pace and momentum to engage and capture your reader's attention. Developing an action story to design your solution for change is an easy way to mobilize your vision.

Understand the value of appropriate action and pace. This means ensuring that the facts and processes of doing something support achieving a specific purpose. Action should be goal-oriented in order to add value. Maintain a steady pace and strive to reach each benchmark so the plan continues to develop and move forward.

Recognize the impact of deeds, motivations, and behaviors. Understanding a person's feelings and thoughts is important, but it is more effective for progress to focus on the behaviors manifested by those thoughts, feelings and motivations.

Focus on the goals of the community. In the story of change, the protagonist is the community or people your solution is ultimately serving. Your goals should be their goals. Your solution should be the solution that adds value to their lives. It is possible for goals and solutions to align, but the actions and pace you set should reflect the priorities of the community.

Maintain appropriate setting that is relevant to the action. Keeping the setting relevant in creating change means ensuring you are considering all the elements, resources, programs and services that exist within the environment you are working in. Leveraging the abundance of existing resources, collaborating with community partners and organizations, and identifying solutions that are sustainable within that environment are critical to ensuring meaningful, relevant and lasting change.

Set off chains of reaction. Being committed to the change has the potential to create ceaseless chains of cause and effect. Leading transformative change that is meaningful should lead to actionable, relevant and sustainable solutions, but it is important to consider the points of connection between the issue and how they interplay with policies, systems and environment (PSE).

Talk is cheap, but actions speak volumes. It is much easier, and considerably safer, to talk about doing something than it is to actually put forth the effort and execute. There are a lot of people out there that live in these safe spaces, yet do not have the courage to cross the street. A great idea without any action behind it will always be just an idea and sooner or later, someone else with the courage to act may have the same idea. Studies from a survey of executive leaders from nearly 200 companies showed that their firms only achieved 63% of the expected results from their strategic plans. The most significant contributor to these results indicated failure to execute as the principal reason for the gap between intentions and outcomes. If you are going to spend the time to dream and form a vision for the future, it is crucial that you have the courage to overcome your fears, worries, and anxieties. Don't be afraid to cross the street, and when you do, make sure you lead as many people as you can and look both ways.

PERPETUAL PERSEVERANCE

BE RESILIENT

"She was unstoppable,

Not because she did not have failures or doubts,

But because she continued on despite them."

-Beau Taplin

How do you deal with difficult circumstances in your life? The stress and anxiety you experience in your work, worry and difficulty you encounter with family and friends, illness and fatigue, world events and traumatic situations all have an effect on you and determine how well you perform and progress in life. Typically, people adapt to evolving and unexpected situations well and find ways to continue to move forward. The ease with which you move forward is determined by your resiliency to change. Resiliency is defined as "the capacity to recover quickly from difficulties." It does not mean that you are immune to feeling the effects of stress and difficulties, but rather your ability to bounce back from the challenges they present. It is your "toughness" that allows you to persist in spite of roadblocks, setbacks and challenges that impedes your path forward. It is in your resiliency that you discover the courage you have inside, the strength of your heart, and the power of your purpose.

Studies have shown that people are more resilient than commonly thought and there are a number of contributing factors that can affect your resilience. According to the University of Chicago's National Opinion Research Center, 92% of Americans have reported experiencing at least one significant negative event in their life. These experiences range from divorce, losing their job, injury or illness to more traumatic events like depression, anxiety, substance abuse, or sexual assault. A study conducted by the National Institute of Nursing Research in 2015 identified two key factors that contributed to a person's ability to be resilient when faced with adverse circumstances: mastery and social support. Both of these factors, as the research found, is completely within our power to control. The first, mastery, depends on how we perceive our ability to control and influence the circumstances that surround us. Not to be confused with optimism, mastery actually lessens the negative effects of bad experiences and is attributed to greater quality of life and health. When I was diagnosed with Post-Traumatic Stress Disorder, or PTSD, in 2013, it was an answer to deep-seated and long-standing behavioral health issues I had been struggling with for several years. While the diagnosis provided an answer, I was left with very little understanding of how to live fully and to be successful despite my disability. Over the years, I have learned to adapt and function in my public and professional life, largely from developing mastery skills to attenuate my symptoms and find moments of restful alertness. Most recently, I have found that meditation is a powerful tool to calm my nerves, quiet my mind and feel less stressed. These methods are forms of self-control and actualization that can help to regain power over your own domain.

Another important factor is having strong social support. This increases your ability to recover and persevere in the face of challenges by having caring and supportive relationships with people that provide love, trust, and offer encouragement and reassurance. My wife, an Army veteran and Registered Nurse, has been amazingly supportive and exhibited unearthly strength and resilience over the years of dealing with my PTSD, as well as her own, and some of the behavioral outbursts and manifestations that stem from that trauma. In the months following my separation from my previous employer, having positive and supportive relationships with my family, friends, and colleagues allowed me to weather the stress and anxiety caused by the legal and administrative fallout with greater grace and ease than if I had been alone with my thoughts and self-doubt. Having a positive social support system in place is proven to reduce the likelihood that one develops psychiatric issues as a result of trauma. Studies have found that discouraging open communication and suppressing memories can cause individuals to become withdrawn, disengaged or blame themselves for the trauma they experience.

Other factors include the ability to establish realistic goals and carry out plans, having positive self-esteem and confidence in their own abilities, effective communication skills and the ability to problem-solve, strong emotional intelligence, and the ability to manage personal feelings and impulses. Cultural differences, personal traumas and experiences contribute to how you communicate feelings, display anxieties, or act out when in distress. This is especially important to understand when considering the resilience of community members, you may work with to ensure you approach them with empathy and an appreciation for cultural diversity.

An organization called the Acumen Fund is a nonprofit venture fund that is tackling poverty through entrepreneurial approaches. One of their programs, the Global Fellows Program, deploys fellows to various countries around the globe to work with and support investee companies to solve intractable problems. In addition to providing financial and business operations training, Acumen also trains fellows to develop a "moral imagination" to help find balance in opposing values in order to see the world as it is presently, and to visualize a better version of what it could be. The aim is to form leaders that have strong business acumen, deep self-awareness, and the resiliency to overcome complex challenges in order to bring about transformative social change.

> *"It is in resiliency that you discover the courage you have inside, the strength of your heart, and the power of your purpose."*

Resilience itself is complex, varying in how it manifests across different domains of life, and may change over time. An example is someone who is very resilient in a high-stress or fast-paced work environment but exhibits a diminished ability to cope with changes in personal or relationship matters. The good thing is that resiliency is not something that you either have or you don't. It is a skill that can be honed and developed over time and with experience, however, there is no "one size fits all" approach. Each person is different, and the way that you build resilience may not work for someone else. Fortunately, there are tools available that have been developed to measure and assess resilience in individuals. In 2003, while working with patients experiencing PTSD, Kathryn M. Connor and R.T.

Davidson developed the Connor-Davidson Resilience Scale (CD-RISC), which was designed to assess and improve upon existing measures and perceived stress. There are 25 items that are divided into the following five factors:

- Personal competence, high standards, and tenacity
- Trust in one's instincts, tolerance of negative affect, and strengthening effects of stress
- Positive acceptance of change and secure relationships
- Control
- Spiritual influence

Connor and Davidson also determined that resiliency can be measured in people through the existence of certain characteristics. These characteristics include:

- Viewing change as an opportunity
- Being committed to the change at all costs
- Engaging the support of others
- Recognizing the limits of control
- Fostering close interpersonal relationships

- Pursuing personal or collective goals
- Maintaining self-efficacy
- Leveraging stress as strength
- Remaining confident in your strengths and abilities
- Using choices to maintain control
- Finding humor in all situations
- Being action-oriented
- Practicing patience
- Tolerant of negativity in an effort to understand
- Adaptable to change
- Cautiously optimistic
- Having faith in a higher power

> *"The greatest difference in the ability to enact change between someone with great vision and inspiring words, and someone who has passion and the courage to act comes down to resilience"*

Viewing this list, we can see that many of the characteristics of resiliency are the same traits associated with a change maker. Having the ability affect change and lead others through transformative social improvement initiatives will require resilience, tenacity, trust in yourself and others, and a steadfast commitment to your purpose. The greatest difference in the ability to enact change between someone with great vision and inspiring words, and someone who has passion and the courage to act comes down to resilience.

As a change maker, you can build resilience during the challenging stages of transition by recognizing what you have the ability to control, and what you do not. Steve Maraboli said, *"Incredible change happens in your life when you decide to take control of what you do have power over instead of craving control over what you don't."* Make a conscious effort to let go of stress, worry, and anxiety over forces that you are not able to influence or restrain. You can begin to do this by realizing that stress and anxiety are not always associated with bad things or impending doom. Anxiety can be an indicator that something amazing is about to happen and it may bring an opportunity to move outside of your own comfortable space. Leading and affecting positive change can cause you to feel anxious and excited because you know something is on the horizon, you just don't know exactly what it will look like. You can begin to manage these feelings by acknowledging what makes you feel uneasy or anxious. Explore all possibilities, identify all the "worst-case" scenarios and write them down. Analyze these objectively and honestly, and then cross off the ones that probably will not happen. For anything that remains, ask yourself if it is something you can live with. Breathe through your thoughts and, as you inhale, think of all the negative items on your list that cause you to worry and stress. As you exhale, push these stressors out of your mind and body with your breath. Visualize them leaving with the same force and speed of your exhalation. When you do this, you may begin to feel lighter as if the weight of these thoughts and feelings were significant on your shoulders and with a simple breath, the fog has been lifted and you are free to focus on more positive thoughts and actions. After you are done, put the list aside and move on to the next task on your list. Keep the note as a reminder for when you have executed and accomplished your goal and use it as a reminder that anxieties do not have to be our realities if we do not allow them to be.

Know your strengths and leverage them as the gifts and talents they are for you and your success, and for how you can share them with the world around you. Studies have shown that people are happier, more engaged and more likely to succeed when they know and play to their strengths. Only when you understand what your strengths are, will you be able to make the changes necessary to find personal fulfillment. The High5

Test is an excellent, free tool that you can use to identify your strengths, as well as, learn how you best fit into a team dynamic. You can access the High5 Test by going to high5test.com. Mindset is everything and when you develop a growth mindset, you may begin to welcome challenges, use criticism as an opportunity to improve, and embrace obstacles to progress as training maneuvers to persist through, and to become stronger; more agile.

One of the most powerful tools I use for mindfulness is meditation, and as I mentioned earlier, has helped a great deal with calming the symptoms of PTSD, OCD and anxiety, quieting my thoughts, and allowing me to be present within myself in the moment. This is much easier said than done, and I often become distracted by the sound of my kids playing, the ticking clock, my Ring doorbell notification, or even my own thoughts that burst into my consciousness. This is okay and it happens to the best of us. Don't allow the noise to distract you from the whole experience. Quiet these noises and push them back by focusing on your breathing. As a devout and practical Catholic, I use this as an opportunity to pray, to thank God for the blessings He has provided, and to ask for clarity and wisdom in overcoming my challenges. Religion is a wonderful source for contemplation and guidance, but you do not have to be spiritual to discover the calm and comfort that comes with quiet meditation.

Next, be aware of the environment that surrounds you. We all lead busy lives and find ourselves consumed by, and dependent on, the noise and chaos of the world. Social media and smart phones, tools that are meant to make us more connected and efficient, often have the opposite effect by distracting us from what we should be focusing on. To refocus your mind, concentrate on the things that surround you in this moment. Pay attention to where you are and what is in the room around you. Are you at home? In your office? How does the floor feel under your feet? How does the air feel or smell? Are there people around you? Who are they? Can you hear the noise outside? Traffic on the streets? Birds singing?

When you do this, you may begin to decipher a rhythm and melody within the noise.

Slow down in your life and in your mind. As busy as we can get, and as good at multi-tasking as you may be, operating at a heightened pace can cause you to feel overwhelmed, frustrated and ineffective and can actually be averse to progress. When you are distracted by a phone call, someone coming into your office, or some other type of interruption, it is important to acknowledge it, address the matter, if need be, and then redirect your attention back to your task.

Lastly, don't be too hard on yourself, or your thoughts. It is normal to have thoughts that you may immediately regret having. Being mindful means that you recognize that your thoughts and feelings do not define who you are as a person. Negative, self-deprecating, or judgmental thoughts are common, but they eventually dissipate. When you are aware of them, and you acknowledge them, you can make a conscience effort to not act upon them, but rather allow them to pass.

Practicing mindfulness provides a unique opportunity to reflect on yourself, your successes, and your path forward as a way of anticipating setbacks and challenges, and to bask in the serenity of the present. It can also have a positive impact on your mental, emotional, and physical health, as well as improve your ability to focus, think creatively, enhance your resiliency, and strengthen your relationships with others.

BE DISCIPLINED

"Everyone must choose between two pains:

The pain of discipline

Or the pain of regret"

-Jim Rohn

When you reflect on your life or your work, consider the reason that you have not been able to achieve the success you had hoped for, affected the change you wanted to, or realized the level of happiness and satisfaction that comes from reaching your goals. There may be several reasons, and, hopefully, if you have read the previous chapters, you have begun to identify some of them. But no matter what the reason, if you ask yourself "but, why" enough times, you may realize that it has to do with discipline. The single most important attribute that distinguishes between the greats and the average is discipline. Without discipline, you would not be driven, or feel the burning desire to succeed. Discipline is the foundation for hard work. No one has ever achieved anything for himself or herself, which did not already exist, without hard work. Your drive is the force momentum that moves you forward at all costs and to put in the hours necessary to make your dream a reality. Being singularly focused on your dream, your goal, or objectives requires discipline to remain committed, to push aside distractions and silence the noise, and compel yourself forward.

We often hear about overnight success stories, but overnight success does not manifest itself. People do not simply emerge out of thin air and instant success by taking the easy route has never existed. The people that seem to have risen to the top out of anonymity, all came from a place where hard work, dedication, perseverance and discipline were necessary to achieve their goals. As changemakers, we sometimes have the deck stacked against us and we have to put in the work, sometimes extraordinarily hard work, to bring about change that is important and necessary.

> 'Discipline committed leads to goals achieved and success sustained.'

If you want to succeed in your life, if you want to achieve great things for yourself and for others, you must be willing to work harder than everyone else. When everyone else says enough, you say more. When others stop to take a break, you continue forward. When you get tired, when you get hurt, when you feel the pain and fatigue from the weight of the work you are carrying, you have to keep moving because there is no other way to success. And when you experience setbacks or barriers, you have to find a way around them. When you get knocked down, use the pain, discomfort, and embarrassment to build your resilience and strengthen your character. If you fall down, get up, learn from what made you stumble so that you can anticipate and dodge it in the future. Discipline is about putting in the amount of work necessary to achieve your goals and make your dream become a reality. Without discipline, you cannot realize sustained change. Critically acclaimed author and journalist, Malcolm Gladwell, wrote in his book 'Outliers: The Story of Success', that "success is a function of persistence and doggedness and the willingness to work hard for twenty-two minutes to make sense of something that most people would give up on after thirty seconds." The time you dedicate to something determines what you will get out of it. Spend little or no time; you get nothing. Commit several hours to understanding, practicing, and excelling and you will develop an asset that is uniquely yours forever.

If you want a change to occur in your life, you have the power to create that change through the choices you make in each present moment of every day. When I founded nLab and started working from home, I decided

I wanted to wake up every morning at 4:00 am and go through a personal daily ritual of prayer, coffee, reading, and getting a head start on work before the chaos of packing lunches, ironing uniforms, and getting the kids ready for school. As I do with all of my ideas and intentions, I told my wife that this is what I was going to do. The first reason was so she didn't worry that something was wrong if she noticed I was not in bed in the wee hours of the morning. The second is because there is no one that would give me a harder time for failing to live up to my own goal than my wife. The point is, when you tell others the change you wish to make, you suddenly feel a sense of accountability to someone other than yourself to follow through. In fact, this is, in essence, a feeling of moral obligation that I can attribute as the rationale for many decisions and choices I make in life. When you are responsible for your choices, own the results of those choices, and use those results to make better choices, you can directly influence the trajectory of who you are and the direction you are moving in. When you make poor choices, when you ignore the consequences of your decisions, and when you lose sight of your purpose, you fail. You fail at reaching your goals, you fail the people who rely on you reaching your goals, and worst of all, you fail yourself. This failure can cause you to lose confidence in your ability to succeed and fills your head with self-deprecating thoughts that, like a cancer, spread to every thought you have. These thoughts will try to convince you that you are not good enough, strong enough, smart enough, educated, or old, or young, or wealthy, or tall, or man, or white, or straight enough to be successful. But the voice is wrong. The voice is your inner self that has become comfortable and content with the status quo. Perhaps the status quo has even provided a measure of prosperity that you have become accustomed to. That voice doesn't mind if things stay the same or if they never change because change is hard and being comfortable is, well, comfortable. Being comfortable and careful is easy and safe. But the easy path rarely leads to success, and never leads to progress. Denzel Washington said in an acceptance speech, "ease is the greater threat to progress than hardship". Without sacrifice *now*, without hard work *now*, and without discipline *now*, you will never achieve the change you desire or reach the success you dream of.

Keep your eye on the prize and continue working even when the results don't seem within reach. Stay focused and your time will come. Change is a slow process. It takes time to undo the effect of all the bad habits and poor choices that have become entrenched in and around your life. But if you want to envision what your life will look like in the next ten years, look at what you are doing today to get there. Have you identified your purpose? Do you have a vision to serve your purpose? Have you set goals to achieve that vision and what are you doing to actively pursue those goals? Who are the people around you that either help or hinder your pursuits? Are you putting in the necessary efforts to achieve your goals or are you resting and waiting for a miracle?

Mahatma Gandhi, a man who was as disciplined in virtually every area of his life as he was principled, said, "be the change you wish to see in the world." People, who change themselves, change the world. Invest in yourself through hard work, dedication, and perseverance and you will be the change that has a lasting impact on the world.

FIND YOUR TRIBE

"A group needs only two things to be a tribe: a shared interest and a way to communicate."

-Seth Godin

There is something about being around other people who share the same interests, ideas, and beliefs that provides a sense of energy, optimism, and belonging. As mentioned previously, relationships are important, but they are also a natural part of being human. We all have an innate desire to belong. The need for connectedness and to feel love is evident in Maslow's hierarchy of needs' motivational theory, specifically contained in the third slice of the pyramid.

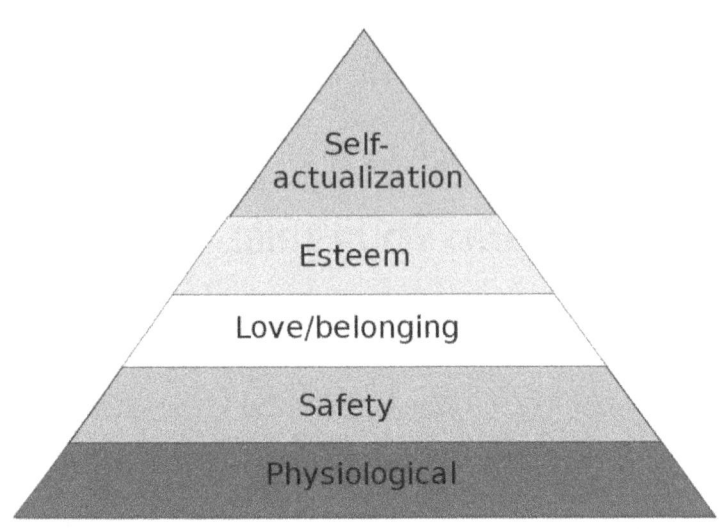

In fact, before one can begin to feel accomplished and, ultimately, achieve their full potential, they must satisfy the need for acceptance, trust, and affiliation. Humans are social creatures that thrive on interaction with others and being accepted by society, so it is understandable that in order to affect real, meaningful and necessary change, we would first need to form the bond of kinmanship and community with those whom we seek the change for, and with.

Gathering a "tribe" of like-minded individuals that share the same dreams and live a similar purpose is paramount to feeling a sense of safety, confidence and self-awareness. Seth Godin, an entrepreneur and author of *'Tribes: We Need You to Lead Us'*, establishes that tribes form based on shared values and ideas to create the power of collective leadership that leads to massive change. He argues that it is this community of like-minded people that influence the greatest change in the world through being interconnected to one another, connected to the leaders, and connected by a shared purpose.

> *Being a leader in change means having the ability to persevere and the courage to face failure*

One of the most important lessons from Godin's book is this: "if your organization requires success before commitment, it will never have either." Too often we are more in love with the idea of being self-important or being included in the discussion than we are truly committed to the change, or even understanding the imperative for it. Being a leader in change means having the ability to persevere, the courage to face failure, to not be great on the journey, but to strive for greatness as a result and to lead others along that perilous and treacherous path. The method for which organizations typically approach change initiatives is not much different from how they approach everything: through hierarchy. For traditional leaders, the standard organizational tree seen across the corporate landscape is a safe and comfortable way to structure efforts to ensure communication, and commands, filter down from a central decision-making authority. Besides the more obvious flaws in a "top-down" approach, the hierarchal structure actually creates barriers to how information is disseminated. By having multiple points of connection that information is required to flow through before arriving at its final intended destination, information can quickly become congested, distorted, or manipulated. Built-in redundancies within this type of system stifle creativity and innovative thinking, and hampers change, allowing status quo to prevail. More to the point, it is not a system that allows people to coalesce, connect and collaborate.

Where change has most often prevailed is within systems outside of traditional hierarchal control. For example, Google, Adobe and LinkedIn have all implemented "flatarchies", a hybrid organizational structure that combine the layers of flatter systems while also allowing ad hoc flat teams to come together and ideate. This flexibility has provided the opportunity for team members to be seen as equals, enabling the company to be nimble and innovate products and services. Holacracy is another model that positions individual employees around roles and specific projects. Employees' job titles are defined by their roles, and groups come together and close as projects form. Zappos and the David Allen Company have implemented holacracy, however, at this point, it appears the model would be more effective in smaller organizations than in large corporations.

> *Identifying your tribe begins with knowing yourself, understanding what you need in your life, and aligning your collective efforts*

These social systems are made up of people at different levels, disciplines, and authorities. All members of the group participate in a shared leadership model; with each person feeling empowered to express their thoughts and beliefs, share their ideas and be genuine stewards for change. This group of like-minded individuals can be either formal or informal. Sometimes, it begins with friendships that span several years. Other times, it may be your schoolmates or colleagues connected by a shared experience or common cause. However, these relationships may form, it is important that they do. Surrounding yourself with supportive and encouraging people is essential to unlocking your inner strength and power to be actionable, resilient and focused on what you strive to achieve. For many people, the ability to attract and connect with others comes naturally, while some may have to work at being vulnerable and exposed. Whether you are introverted or extroverted, identifying your tribe begins with knowing yourself, understanding what you need in your life, and aligning your collective efforts to support, encourage, and uplift each other.

Knowing who you are, what you are passionate about, and understanding your purpose in life is key to recognizing the energy you need from within others. Knowing yourself means being comfortable with who you are and allowing that self-confidence to act as a magnet, attracting others that seek similar connections. This self-confidence ensures that change only occurs from within you, as you grow, learn, and evolve as a person and not simply because you wish to fit in with a particular person or group. A genuine tribe should foster a sense of value, respect, and genuine compassion and be accepting of the unique differences and colors each member brings.

Next, it is equally important to understand what, and who, you need. This means that some people may not make the cut. This may include family members, friends, neighbors, or coworkers, and while it does not mean that you have to disown your family, move to a different side of town, or quit your job, but it does mean that you need to be aware of the qualities that you seek in others, as well as those that conflict or challenge the changes you seek within yourself. You have to ask yourself, and be willing to listen, what qualities and characteristics are you looking for in others? Are you seeking a friend, a mentor, or a teacher? Are you looking for someone that can provide emotional support or provide a "head-check" when you are too close or consumed by an issue? Do you need a partner to exchange ideas and seek solutions? Is there something that you wish to know more about and seek a mentor to coach and guide you? Understanding what you need is key to ensuring you attract the people that will be most valuable and beneficial to helping you achieve your goals.

Les Brown, famous motivational speaker and author, says that it is important to "align yourself with people that you can learn from, people who want more out of life, people who are stretching and searching and seeking some higher ground in life." A common analogy of alignment is to think of a flock of geese flying in formation, migrating several thousand miles per day against the odds of weather and wind resistance in order to arrive together in warmer climate. Geese understand that as the seasons change, they too must adapt in order to survive and thrive. They align their efforts, flying in a formation that takes advantage of the windbreak from the birds in front, minimizing resistance and easing the efforts of each member of the flock. When considering your tribe, you must also think about how each member's characteristics, strengths, and skills can contribute and align with the rest of the group. This includes understanding the unique strengths that each person brings, sharing in the leadership responsibilities to protect each member from fatigue and burnout, maintaining clear and open lines of communication to ensure consistent forward momentum, fostering a culture of accountability and trust, and ensuring the group is always purpose-driven, remaining focused on the shared vision and outcomes.

> *Only within community can we grow beyond ourselves*

Finding and engaging your tribe allows you to leverage the power of collective action, to coalesce around core values, and to encourage, support, and propel each other forward. Only within community can we grow beyond ourselves. Transformative change requires the combined efforts of many to be greater than the sum of all their parts. It will be this collective action that changes the world. Not wealth. Not industry. Not politics. Tribes. More simply, people.

"As an organizer I start from where the world is, as it is, not as I would like it to be. That we accept the world as it is does not in any sense weaken our desire to change it into what we believe it should be – it is necessary to begin where the world is if we are going to change it to what we think it should be."

- Saul Alinsky, Rules for Radicals

CLOSING THOUGHT

The starting point for change is where you are. Where you are in your life. Where your community is. Where your country or the world or the state of the problem you seek to improve is. Meet it where it is today. Defining the problem, understanding how it perpetuated the reality that exists, allows us to better understand who and what is needed to deconstruct, reverse-engineer, and unravel the ties that bind us to status quo and give us the freedom to innovate, create, and thrive.

Good luck and God Speed my fellow Changemakers!

ACKNOWLEDGEMENTS

I would like to take an opportunity to thank everyone that has contributed to this book, either through our interactions over the years, our partnership and shared passion for improving people's lives, and even for those who have taught the invaluable lessons learned through each challenging experience and conflict. I have learned so much from many of you on how to be, and who to be, and for what purpose.

A special thanks to the wonderful board members at nLab Concepts, who have provided such amazing and invaluable advice, guidance, and support as we started the organization, discovered our vision, and formulated our approach to addressing systemic issues and advancing opportunities for equity and inclusion.

To Simon, the man who painstakingly combed through the pages of a manuscript that was, in its earliest phases, a rough manifesto of incoherent thoughts and idealistic notions, yet through his keen eye, skillful literary genius, and a shared sense of passion for progressive change transformed these pages into something beautiful and unique.

And finally, and certainly most importantly, to my wonderful wife, partner and best friend, Kim, who has demonstrated patience and understanding as she graciously read each word and struggled over each poorly formed sentence structure, grammatical error, and ramblings of this book in its roughest drafts. The amount of courage, character, resilience and grace she has shown me in her life, and in ours together, has been a source of personal inspiration.

www.ingramcontent.com/pod-product-compliance
Lightning Source LLC
LaVergne TN
LVHW041251080426
835510LV00009B/697